# THE CONFIDENCE CONTINUUM

*Gratitude:*

*Theresa Malone, my mother and first confidence teacher*
*My grandmothers, aunts (the real divas), sister, close friends, and cousins*
*I am so blessed to have a supportive and loving family*
*My niece, Elie, the youngest participant within this body of work*
*The Milwaukee Center for Children and Youth*
*Anita O'Conor, my mentor and clinical supervisor during graduate school who has
consistently pushed me and supported me from the beginning of this journey*
*Thank you to all the participants in the last three years!*
*I believe that I have learned more about confidence from you than you have from me.*
*Finally, my wish is to build an honorable altar to God, for confidence is about truly
believing that you are who God says that you are!*

*"Your life isn't about a big break.*

*It's about taking one significant life-transforming step at a time."*
*-Oprah Winfrey*

*"The Confidence Class provided my daughters with support and encouragement to use their voice, be kind to and love themselves. After completing the class, I saw my girls applying some of the concepts learned and continuing to do so in their everyday lives. One daughter said, 'It helped me to see things about myself that I didn't see before.'"*

*"My daughter started the confidence program at 11 years old. She was in her first year of middle school and needed more positive mentors and peers. I appreciated the program and how it acknowledged her presence, to just let them exist, and gave them the freedom to define themselves. Just having multiple positive woman influences will go a long way to a young minority woman's life. Her going to this program once a month is a perfect example of a great self-care day, which is important for a young woman, and to have people who want to assist in the well-being of my daughter and teaching her to appreciate herself for who she is and help encourage her personal growth. This program helps young women acknowledge and appreciate themselves with recognition, which creates self-acceptance and helps strengthen self-esteem. This will create more women minority leaders."*

*"The Confidence Class not only helps our girls build their confidence but breaks down the biases towards black girls by giving them the tools to keep going, no matter what obstacles may come their way. This class has taught my daughter the importance of relationships, speaking up, and being proud of who she is. Jovan does great activities with the girls to get them to understand that they are precious and special in their own way."*

*"My daughter attended the Confidence Class since its conception, and we loved it! My daughter has always been bright and full of joy but needed the extra boost to have her own voice. I think that the starting ages for this class are great because the young ladies are leaving the 'baby' stage and entering the 'big girl' stage. My daughter was able to see other black and brown women in leadership roles, and this is another reason I loved it. Jovan Goodman did a wonderful job exposing the girls to our community, world, and themselves. Those introductions will last a lifetime. As a parent this was just a Saturday program for her to have something to do, yet it was a safe space for her to learn and a judgment-free zone for her to express herself."*

# Contents

**Facilitators Guide**

## Activities

# Background

The Confidence Continuum was created while developing and facilitating various trauma-informed evidence-based programming as a graduate student at a nonprofit organization for teen girls and young women. I desired to create something fun and to work with younger girls in hopes of transitioning to more preventative work. I created this class for a 6- to 12-year old age range. However, there are times that teens and adults joined and found the activities extremely helpful. My hope is that all women will somehow be inspired by this work.

All too often interventions are created to reduce or discontinue undesirable behavior. I don't know if that is why I created the Confidence Class. My hope is to build an awareness within all girls who participate in this program. My hope is that awareness and engaging in meaningful activity will produce a greater understanding of self that is sustainable long term. Within the three years that this class was presented to girls in a community setting, we observed enhanced levels of confidence demonstrated both in this class and in school settings, according to testimonials from parents.

Confidence is on a continuum or scale in which some of us may never be "a complete 10" every day or have full indisputable confidence. I like to think of it as a journey instead of a destination. The activities in this class will build an awareness with the hope of providing tools when girls need them the most so that they will be able to turn to them for future reflection and possible behavior modification. Lastly, creating a community that is fun and safe is important for girls everywhere. Seeing other girls in community allows them to learn from each other and build relational trust. Girls around the world often suffer from similar social issues: inequality in education, bullying, colorism, image shaming, etc. This class is designed to create a larger community of support for girls tackling these issues globally.

# Perspective

As a little black girl from the east side of Milwaukee, Wisconsin, I was raised by a single mother who obtained a great deal of support from maternal and paternal relatives. Growing up, I spent a great deal of time with my grandparents, attending church and senior citizen events within my community. I was raised in a family that supported my personal confidence and image. However, as I grew up and had different experiences in grade school and high school, I began to struggle, at times, with body image and colorism issues that were deeply rooted within my community and environment like so many other girls around the world. In high school, I began modeling, which enhanced my individual concept and understanding of beauty. As a young adult, I continued to experience moments in my life that shaped my perspective and ideas for what tools and support women need and desire to personally thrive. Many of the concepts and activities within this curriculum are inspired by my personal experiences traveling, spending time with family, employment in the modeling industry, and my work serving women and girls in both professional and private settings.

# Core Objectives

1. To build personal awareness within girls.
2. To enhance confidence by the introduction and completion of the detailed activities through self-expression and art.
3. To foster community building; because women and girls are so relational, presenting them with opportunities to build awareness and enhance confidence within their community with other girls provides a greater opportunity for both shared and transferred learning and success.

# The Confidence Scale

The confidence scale is a scale from 1 to 10 to which the girls will be introduced throughout the class as a necessary tool for monitoring progress and positive outcomes for continuous program evaluation. Its purpose is also to build awareness for the participants and collect meaningful data regarding outcomes. The idea is that the numbers on the scale are utilized and referenced to reflect how the girls feel about their confidence or self-esteem at the beginning and end of each class:

1: "I do not feel so confident at all."

Girls may be feeling worthless and unable to find any positive things to say about themselves.

10: "I am feeling very confident and can think of many positive attributes that I have in this moment."

5: May be a combination of both feelings indicated above.

Other numbers within the scale should be captured and recorded. The scale will be referred to throughout the class. Participants should be encouraged to identify with a sticker or marker at the beginning and end of each day. Ensure that this process is safe and confidential. It is useful to have a large laminated copy of the scale for continued usage. Overseer must record data from the scale at the beginning and end of the day to monitor process.

All participants should be introduced to this scale and clearly understand its usage, purpose, and meaning behind each score. Usage of this scale by all participants will suggest a daily awareness of confidence, esteem, and general well-being. After the discussions and activities, the scale will determine learned skills from the class and test the overall temperature of the community. If there is a concern for confidentiality or validity due to group dynamics, please adjust to an individual scale for each participant to use daily and record.

*If this curriculum is not being delivered in a group context and this data is not needed for program outcomes, please decide if it is appropriate. There is an optional scale within each activity for personal use.

**Additional Components and Structure**

**Discussion:** Short time periods where participants engage in dialogue about the daily topic. Key questions are provided for discussion; however, the coach of the group should facilitate and offer additional questions that contribute to the nature of the conversation at any given time. Discussion also leads to deep reflection.

**Activity:** An art activity is a fun and beneficial way to engage with the group and encourage expression and creativity. This is not a therapeutic group; however, using art has been beneficial for children in several settings. All the activities include a list of supplies and correlate to the given topic of each day. They are specifically designed to create self-reflection during the process. In addition, many activities can return home with the participant as a helpful future tool. There are opportunities to complete some activities within this book. Facilitators and coaches are encouraged to complete the art activities with the participants.

**Confidence Walk**: This is a time for each girl to have fun and demonstrate an expression of their discussion and art activity with a live confidence walk at the end of every class. Each girl lines up and takes a turn to walk. This is a very uncomfortable process in the beginning of the class, but with encouragement from the coach and other participants, each participant's comfort level increases. Posture and eye contact are key for a great confidence walk, and the coach should feel free to demonstrate that. Because this occurs at the end of each class, please ensure that this is a time when the group verbally supports each other as a closing ritual. (audio device needed with recommended song list)

## Group Management

Facilitator may require information and/or education on classroom/group management. Some activities may provoke individual feelings or emotions that would need to be addressed or supported within the group. This is not intended to serve as a therapeutic intervention; however, if the class is used in such settings, please ensure that licensed professionals are present and/or providing consultation and guidance where needed.

## Implementation Guidance

This curriculum has been facilitated with primarily African American girls. The assumption is that this curriculum will connect well with girls of color as it is written from this perspective. It is believed that this work will translate and benefit other girls and all ethnicities. Global adaptations are encouraged and may require additional consultation.

The duties of a facilitator for a recommended class size of approximately 10 girls include the ability to fully understand the purpose of the program; to naturally and genuinely engage with girls (specifically girls of color); and to understand current societal issues plaguing girls of color such as structural racism and oppression, sexism, and other forms of discrimination. Additional consultation is available to ensure that this curriculum is delivered with the best intention and positive outcomes for girls in communities globally.

## Program-Related Details

The recommendation is to hold this class on a daily to weekly basis in two-hour durations. Every class should include a discussion, art activity, and confidence walk. Snacks are a great addition and help to create community. The program is adaptable and ideal for girls within schools, churches, group homes, therapy centers, and juvenile delinquency centers. An intimate group of 10 girls between the ages of 6 and 12 years is recommended. Adaptations for teen-aged girls and adult women may be appropriate. However, consultation is recommended if that is a desire.

The environment in which this program is facilitated must be experienced with great enthusiasm and positivity. Vibrant colors are important for the atmosphere. An adult serving as a coach to facilitate and monitor the group is recommended; however, the curriculum is meant to foster leadership for girls within the group.

## Optional Items

Strobe light for welcome

Red carpet for confidence walks

## Optional Supplemental Activities

Career Day

Mother/Daughter (Introduces importance of generational confidence to group. Parents who transport child from the class often join Confidence Walk at the end.)

Poetry

Yoga

Nia

## Innovation

Please feel free to foster creativity and innovation through this group and to cater to the needs of the participants when necessary. Please feel free to consult when necessary or if unsure.

Deciding whether rules or agreements are needed for the group should be decided by the gr...

# Recommended Playlist for Confidence Walks

Alicia Keys "Girl on Fire"

India Arie "Not Your Average Girl" and "Strength, Courage, and Wisdom"

Rihanna "Diamonds"

Cyndi Lauper "Girls Just Want to Have Fun"

Beyoncé "Brown Skin Girl"

Katy Perry "Roar"


Additional guidance available on www.jovangoodman.com

**Activity #1**

**Welcome to the Confidence Class**

Introduce the concept of confidence to the participants. There are several ideas that participants will have. The job of the facilitator is not to ever operationally define confidence for the group but to manage the process of discovery for each person. Essentially, confidence is whatever the participant understands or agrees to within reason.

## Discussion Questions

What is confidence?

What does confidence mean to you?

Name one person who represents confidence to you and explain why.

Are there any verbal cues or nonverbals you notice that are related to confidence?

Discuss a time when you felt your most confident.

**Introduce Confidence Scale**

Introduce confidence scale to identify where each girl is before and after each class. This is the first class where it is introduced. It will be used at the beginning and ending of every class. Now that confidence has been defined for the group, it will be used at the beginning and end of each subsequent class. Please use the guidance above to define and explain the purpose of the scale. Ensure that the scale is located at a place in the room where the girls feel comfortable using it. Reach agreement on its location, purpose, and usage. If you are not within a group setting, please feel free to utilize the pages to indicate your selection before and after each activity.

1                                                                                              10

**Materials**

Magazines

Markers, crayons, colored pencils

Glue

Poster board

Scissors

Stickers and other fun art supplies are optional

**Directions:**

Each person will receive a poster board with markers, crayons, or colored pencils. Each person will also receive a pair of scissors, glue, and a magazine to select pictures, graphics, and words from. Each person will create their own confidence poster boards, which are clusters of what confidence means for them. Please ask who would like to present and allow each person to have an opportunity. Do not force anyone to present their poster. Solicit feedback and/or questioning where appropriate.

**Confidence Walk:**

Participants are generally somewhat shy the first day but allow those who are interested to demonstrate a confidence walk and encourage other participants to cheer them on. The group may need the facilitator or other young person or adult to model first. Encourage them to practice their confidence walks at home before the next group. See recommended playlist in facilitator's guide.

## Activity #2

### Inner Beauty Vs. Outer Beauty

Participants begin to understand the difference between inner and outer beauty. Participants create a visual and begin to understand how to demonstrate their inner beauty.

**Welcome and Confidence Scale**

1                                                                                          10

## Discussion Questions

What is inner beauty?

What is outer beauty?

Which one would you guess is more important and why?

Who is someone you know who exudes inner beauty? Describe what behaviors you observe about this person.

## Materials

Blank Masks purchased or made from paper

Markers, colored pencils, crayons

Stickers, paint, or other optional art supplies

Glitter or glittered materials

## Directions

Each person will receive a mask with markers, crayons, or colored pencils. Each person will decorate their mask. This works best with masks that include a tie in the back. Participants can put them on after decorating and show them off right away.

## Confidence Walk

Today they will complete their walks while wearing the masks. (This may encourage some who are shy to participate). Instruct them to demonstrate their inner beauty while showing off their walks.

# Activity #3

## My Strengths

Everyone has strengths. The purpose of today's class is to have participants begin to think about what they are good at.

**Welcome and Confidence Scale**

1                                                                                    10

# Discussion

What are strengths?

When did you first learn of a personal strength of yours?

What are you good at that you feel is rare or that no one else is good at?

Think of a time when you were praised for something that you did very well. Share if you choose.

Here are some helpful statement starters:

I wish to be good at_____

I will work to be good at_____

I am good at_____

I am great at_____

I am excellent at_____

I am wonderful when_____

I am most valued for_____

I am unique by_____

I am special because_____

I am my best when_____

**Materials**

Blank 4x6 photo frame made for adding art

Markers and paints to decorate photo frame

Other crafts that would complement décor of photo frame

A 4x6 picture of each participant (optional)

**Directions**

Participants will begin decorating the photo frame with different colors and specific words that describe them and their strengths. Have each participant present their frames. If participants provide pictures of themselves in advance, have them enter the picture in the photo frame after it is decorated and before the presentation. If participants feel comfortable speaking in third person about themselves, this is also acceptable.

**Confidence Walk**

Suggested Music is "Strength, Courage, and Wisdom" by India Irie

INSERT PICTURE

# Activity #4

## Power Affirmations

Power affirmations are statements that produce power and create positive energy to be experienced in life. Verbally stating them out loud can improve self-esteem and confidence in the moment. The purpose is to introduce participants to power affirmations, and they will create their own power affirmation as a bumper sticker during the activity.

**Welcome and Confidence Scale**

1                                                                                    10

## Discussion

Think of one positive statement that you could say daily to help improve your day.

Here are some examples:

Today I choose to be happy

Today I choose to be peaceful

Today I choose to be creative

Today I am creating the reality of what my life will look like

Now, try by finishing these sentences:

Today I_____

Tomorrow I _____

My future is

What impact do you think these statements may have on your day?

## Materials

Blank bumper stickers

Permanent colorful markers

## Directions

Each participant will write their power affirmation statement on a blank bumper sticker. They are free to decorate it if they choose and present to the group. Each person should have a different statement that is unique to them.

## Confidence Walk

Please encourage participants to declare their power affirmations at the end of their confidence walks loud and boldly!

# Activity #5

## Some things are sacred

Sacred boxes are decorative boxes used for keepsakes. Participants may use the sacred boxes to keep items from the activities from this class or any other item that inspires them and represents confidence.

## Welcome and Confidence Scale

1                                                                 10

**Discussion:** Before starting the activity, process what kinds of items may be placed into the sacred box. Typically, these boxes are recommended for things created during this class or other expressions of confidence.

## Materials

5 x 7- or 8 x 12-inch plain boxes or a recycled shoe box

Markers

Stickers

Magazines


## Directions

Each participant receives a box to decorate with colors and inspiring words for keeping all their confidence materials such as sacred poems, affirmations, jewelry, etc. Participants are encouraged to place this box in a special place where they only have access and to use the box to remember what they learned about confidence throughout the class. This box can be used to inspire them when feeling sad, anxious, or even happy. Inside the boxes are reminders of who each girl is and her power to create confidence.


## Confidence Walk

Participants should be more comfortable with "trying on" their walk in the group setting!

# Activity #6

## I am a Queen

Historically, queens have always ruled and been powerful leaders. Because we live in a male patriarchal society, women and girls often don't see those images of themselves. During this activity, each girl will create and decorate her own crown.

## Icebreaker Questions

If you were a queen, what one thing would you change to make the world a better place?

Who would live in your queendom?

What would be the rules in your queendom?

## Supplies needed

Blank paper or foam crowns purchased from a craft store

Markers

Beads and gems

Glue gun

## Directions:

Add color to the crown and beads and gemstones with a glue gun. Don't forget to attach the ends of the crown so that it can be worn during the confidence walks.

## Optional Chant

I am a queen!

I am Amina, the queen of Zaria, Nigeria!

I am Candace, the empress of Ethiopia!

I am Makeda, the queen of Sheba!

I am Nefertiti, the queen of ancient Kemet!

I am Yaa Asantewa of the Ashanti kingdom!

I am a queen!

I am a queen!

I, too, am a queen!
*Repeat*

## Confidence Walk

**Activity #7**

**Confidence Symbols**

This is an introduction to the West African Adinkra symbol for confidence that we will use in the group while recognizing and honoring this important culture.

**Welcome and Confidence Scale**

1                                                                                          10

## Check In

How is everyone feeling about Confidence Class so far?

Do you have any favorite activities? Why?

What is your least favorite activity? Why?

What discussions have you appreciated or learned from?

Now that you have learned more about confidence, have you noticed any symbols that represent confidence for you?

**Additional Directions**

Participants can draw this symbol on other material or use the pages of this book. Use markers, crayons, or colored pencils to decorate your symbol and display to other participants. Please explain what confidence means to you and why you chose the words or colors to decorate your symbol. What are other symbols you see daily of confidence and what do they mean to you?

**Confidence Walk**

Suggested music is "Brown Skin Girl" by Beyoncé Knowles

## Activity #8

### Honor the complexity

Our lives are complex. Learn to love or appreciate the complexities.

**Welcome and Confidence Scale**

1                                                                                                   10

**Supplies needed**

Paper

Pencil

Blank small puzzle purchased from a craft store (optional, if finances permit)

## Directions

Fold a sheet of paper in half. On the right side, draw a picture of yourself from your point of view. How do you see yourself? On the left side, draw a picture of how you believe that others see you. Participants can also use words to describe. Take some time to process how different or similar the pictures or words are to one another. When processing is finished, participants will tear the piece of paper in half, throw away the left side (world view), and keep the right side (personal view). Please provide confidentiality during this exercise.

**Additional Directions**

Participants use a blank mini puzzle or torn sheets of paper into about 5-6 pieces (see below). On each piece of paper or puzzle piece, write different words to describe yourself. If you do not have words, color each piece with different colors of your choice. Practice pulling all the different pieces apart and putting them back together again.

Example:

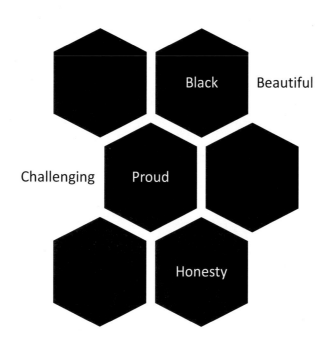

Blank:

**Confidence Walk:**

Take a deep breath with the group in silence for two to three minutes today. Have participants think about what they have shared: their complexities, strengths, and struggles/challenges. This confidence walk is meant to honor them all.  Suggested music is "Roar" by Katy Perry.

# Activity #9

## Life Timeline

Participants reflect on different moments in their lives and where they see their future.

**Welcome and Confidence Scale**

1                                                                                              10

**Supplies**

Paper

Pencil (Colored, optional)

**Directions**

Girls will create a timeline and at each point, write positive moments they have experienced in life. (Examples may include an accomplishment, vacation, or special moment with family) On the back of the sheet of paper or on the bottom, write three things they wish to accomplish further down the timeline or in the future.

## Discussion

What moments stick out the most on your timeline?

Are some moments more important to you than others? Why?

What's on your future timeline?

What will you need to meet those future goals that are on your timeline?

What potential distractions or barriers will keep you from meeting those goals or accomplishments?

What specific attitudes or characteristics must you possess to be successful?

What positive things must you continue doing?

Is there anything about your perspective or attitude that you may want to consider changing?

Are you on track?

What obstacles have you overcome?

Please share if this class or material has helped you to overcome any obstacles in your life.

**Confidence Walk**

## Activity #10
## Writing Prompts
Writing can be a source for creativity, healing, and manifestation.
It's important to teach girls early about the power of writing.

**Welcome and Confidence Scale**

1                                                                                    10

**Supplies**
Paper
Pen/pencil
Journals (Colorful or ones that could be decorated during the class)

**Directions**
Participants will think of their favorite thing to write or talk about and write it on a piece of paper. Collect all the papers together, choose one at a time, and read the topic aloud. Allow about three minutes to write on each topic. Continue until all the topics have been selected and every topic has been written about. This class is dedicated to journaling and should be a silent activity. However, participants can share a journal excerpt of their choice if they desire.

**Confidence Walk**

# Activity #11

## Confidence Recipe

Like most things, there is a recipe. This activity includes a recipe for confidence. After all that has been shared within the group, everyone should have some tools and ideas to create their own recipe. Participants will include the "ingredients" needed for confidence and the directions to share with others. For this activity, incorporating a small and easy food recipe for the group is recommended.

**Welcome and Confidence Scale**

1                                                                                                    10

**Supplies**

Paper

Pen/pencil

Colored pencils for décor are optional

**Directions**

Think about everything you have learned through the activities about confidence at this point. Essentially, everyone has their own recipe for Confidence. Think about what ingredients you need to feel confident daily (Ex: Self-esteem, affirmations, inner beauty, vision, etc.) Write these in the ingredient section. Now, elaborate and complete full sentences about these words or concepts into the directions section. Feel free to share your personal confidence recipe with others. Be as creative as you would like!

# Confidence Recipe

**Preparation time:** _____

**Ingredients:**

_____

_____

_____

_____

_____

**Directions:**

_____

_____

_____

_____

_____

_____

**From the kitchen of:**

**Confidence Walk**

## Activity #12

### Confidence Pledge

This is an opportunity for participants to reflect on what they have learned throughout the class and make a promise to themselves.

**Welcome and Confidence Scale**

Supplies:

Paper

Pencil/Pen

**Directions:**

Have participants begin with "This is my personal pledge to be confident in all I that I do"

Please describe in the lines below what it will look like if you are confident in all you do. Describe your behavior.

Who will know that you are doing "it"?

What will you not be doing?

"When I don't feel as confident, there are things that I can do like_____"

(List three techniques or skills that you learned from the class. Brainstorm with group if necessary)

**Confidence Walk**

## Activity #13

### Confidence Letter

As this series of classes comes to an end, letters should be written for the next group of participants. They will receive these at their first class. If this is not a structured class, please find another girl to give your letter to and tell them about this book!

**Welcome and Confidence Scale**

Supplies:

Stationery paper or use the sheet that has been provided within the book

Pen

Envelopes

Dear Confident Girl,

The top three things that I learned in this class are…

I want to tell you that you are (three adjectives/positive words)

Whenever you need encouragement, please remember to (share three beneficial activities and/or tips learned from the class)

I believe in you.

Signed,

*insert name

# Dear Confident Girl,

_____

_____

_____

_____

_____

_____

_____

_____

_____

_____

_____

_____

_____

**Signed,**

Final Confidence Walk

**Congratulations! You have completed the class!**

**Free downloads for certificate of completion and more at www.jovangoodman.com**

## About the Author

Jovan Goodman is a certified advanced practice social worker and has been working in the social services field for the last ten years in various roles from direct service, management, and macro practice. Jovan has a bachelor's degree in criminal justice from the University of Wisconsin–Parkside and studied abroad as an undergraduate at Stellenbosch University in South Africa. She received her MSW degree with a concentration in child welfare from the University of Wisconsin–Milwaukee.

As a graduate student, Jovan enjoyed partnering with service delivery systems to develop and facilitate evidence-based programming for children and families impacted by trauma in her community.  The inspiration for the Confidence Continuum curriculum was then developed as Jovan wanted to create meaningful prevention programming for younger children.